_____

A gift for

_____

From

_____

Date

A baby is
a little piece of
heaven.

# Blessings
## for Baby

Illustrated by Melissa Babcock Saylor

Published by J. Countryman, a division of Thomas Nelson, Inc., Nashville, Tennessee 37214

Project editor: Terri Gibbs

Designed by Left Coast Design Inc., Portland, Oregon

ISBN: 08499-9601-5

www.thomasnelson.com

Printed in China

Honor is a gift
we give to others.

—Gary Smalley

# Introduction

When we bless others we give them our good wishes and prayers as a gift. We offer words of joy and kindness.

To offer a blessing for another person is to seek to give back a portion of the blessing God has given to us—as well as a portion of the blessing that person has been to us.

When we ask God to bless others, we want them to receive God's good gifts.

What is a blessing? It's a melding of thanksgiving, heart-felt sentiment, and prayer. It can be whimsical, witty, poignant, or prayerful. The words come straight from your heart—words of sincerity and honest affection. Write a wonderful thought for the precious baby. Wish the child a life blessed with love!

Terri Gibbs
Editor

Each time a
child is born
the world
lights up with
new possibilities.

—Florence Schiavo

May your hands reach out to grasp Him,
May your eyes look for His face,
May you smile because you feel Him
Cradle you in His warm embrace.
May the angel glow that lights your face
Never fade to dim,
May your careless giggle
remind us all
That you belong to Him.

—Janelle Chang

# The Day Baby Was Born

_____

Baby's Full Name

_____

Date of Birth

_____

Place of Birth

_____

Time of Birth

_____

Mother's Full Name

_____

Daddy's Full Name

_____

Siblings

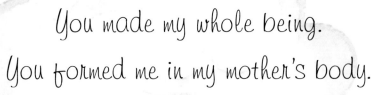

You made my whole being.
You formed me in my mother's body.
I praise you because
you made me
in an amazing and
wonderful way.

Psalm 139:13–14

# Blessed Baby

Weight _____

Height _____

Color of Hair _____

Color of Eyes _____

Mommy thinks you look like _____

_____

Daddy thinks you look like _____

_____

God could not
be everywhere,
so He made mothers.

—Jewish Proverb

# A Special Blessing
## from Mommy

_____

_____

_____

_____

_____

_____

Let us celebrate each child as best,
most adored, most surely blessed.

—Walter Dean Myers

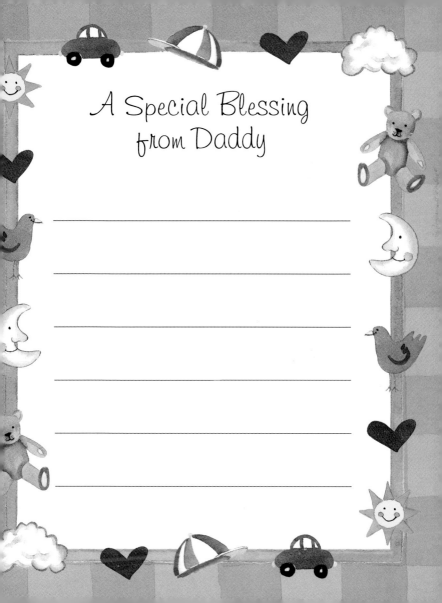

# A Special Blessing from Daddy

_____

_____

_____

_____

_____

_____

Of all the
happy times in life,
a baby's birth
is one of the best!

# A Blessing for Baby

from_____

_____

_____

_____

_____

_____

# Precious Baby's Blessing

God bless you, pure heart,
with aspirations towards ideals.
May you long to strive toward becoming
honest, noble, humble, loyal, selfless,
and diligent. May each of
these ideals be directed by a faith
and love for God.

—Lynette Carnahan Gray

Jesus friend of little children,

Be a friend to me,

Take my hand and ever keep me

Close to thee.

—Walter J. Mathams

# A Blessing for Baby

from_____

_____

_____

_____

_____

_____

I look at the sky so blue and say,
"This is a miracle!"
I look at you, a baby brand new,
and say
"This is a miracle, too!"

# A Blessing for Baby

from _____

Dear Father,
Hear and bless
Thy beasts
And singing birds;
And guard with tenderness
Small things that have
no words.

—Anonymous

Little One,

As you grow through life, from your first baby step to your very last on this earth—may your days be filled with the peace and joy that comes from knowing that with each step you take, you are cradled tenderly in the hand of the eternal Creator.

—Natalie Nichols Gillespie

# A Blessing for Baby

from_____

_____

_____

_____

_____

_____

_____

Where did you come from, Baby dear?
Out of the everywhere into here.

Where did you get your eyes so blue?
Out of the sky as I came through.

Whence that three-corner'd smile of bliss?
Three angels gave me at once a kiss.

But how did you come to us, you dear?
God thought of you, and so I am here.

—George MacDonald

# A Blessing for Baby

from_____

_____

_____

_____

_____

_____

_____

I love little children,
and it is not a light thing
when they, who are fresh
from God, love us.

—Charles Dickens

# A Blessing for Baby

from _____

Babies are
such a nice way
to start people.

—Don Harold

# A Blessing for Baby

from _____

_____

_____

_____

_____

_____

_____

# Baby of My Dreams

I haven't even seen your face.

Yet, I know that you're more beautiful than any dream

I've had of you.

I haven't felt your touch.

But, still, it feels like the

    petals of a flower.

I've never held you in my arms.

But, they're warm with the weight of your tiny body.

I do not know you.

But, I still feel the bond we already share.

You are the child God will bless me with…someday.

Someday.

—Nicole Wilkinson

# A Blessing for Baby

from _____

★ ★ ★

_____

_____

_____

_____

_____

_____

Train up a child in the way he should go,
and when he is old
he will not depart from it.

Proverbs 22:6

What joy is welcomed
like that of a
new born child?

—Caroline Norton

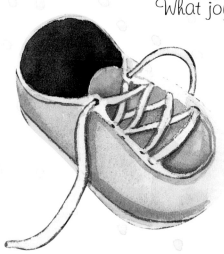

# A Blessing for My Baby Boy

May you grow to be the man your father is, strong, but tender, light-hearted but wise.

May you someday make the girl of your dreams laugh, and hold her gently while she cries.

May you never lose that mischievous gleam, marvelous sense of curiosity, and the sheer pleasure you get from just being alive.

—Natalie Nichols Gillespie

# A Blessing for Baby

from _____

♥  ♥  ♥

_____

_____

_____

_____

_____

_____

There is never a second's loneliness, pushing a baby carriage. Children come rushing up to tag along beside you. Passing people smile and steal a glance.... For who can resist the marvel—a human being still so small that he lies sleeping on his tummy in public?

—Marjorie Holmes

# A Blessing for Baby

from_____

Let the little children come to Me,...

for of such is the kingdom of God.

Mark 10:14

Out of the mouth of babes

and nursing infants

You have ordained strength.

Psalm 8:2

# A Blessing for Baby

from_____

_____

_____

_____

_____

_____

_____

Hush, my dear, lie still and slumber
Holy angels guard they bed!
Heavenly blessings without number
Gently falling on thy head.

—Isaac Watts

# A Blessing for a Little Miracle

Because you were so anxious
To get into this world,
You'll have to struggle a little harder
Than other baby boys and girls.

Every breath becomes a blessing.
The next heartbeat is a goal.
The simple things we take for granted
Take all your heart and soul

God has heard our every prayer
And sent an angel down
To love you and protect you
When we can't be around.

We love you, Little Miracle.
We just ask "do your best."
Please grow strong and healthy,
And know that you are blessed.

—Amy Parker

# A Blessing for Baby

from _____

Some of the grandest miracles
come in the smallest of ways.

—Jamie Hunter

There is no friendship,
no love, like that of
the parent for the child.

—Henry Ward Beecher

# A Blessing for Baby

from_____

❀ ❀ ❀

_____

_____

_____

_____

_____

_____

# The birth of a baby is something to celebrate!

# A Blessing for Baby

from_____

_____

_____

_____

_____

_____

_____

Blessed sweet baby,
Child of this day,
We've so few months
to hold you
Until you go out
to play.

# A Blessing for Baby

from _____

_____

_____

_____

_____

_____

God made the sun
  And God made the tree,
God made the mountains
  And God made me.

I thank you, O God,
  For the sun and the tree,
    For making the mountains
      And for making me.

—Leah Gale

# A Blessing for Baby

from _____

♥ ♥ ♥

_____

_____

_____

_____

_____

# A Blessing for Baby Jordan

One year ago today, you were small and helpless in my arms; dependent on me for everything. Today, you are a vibrant, happy bundle of energy, already searching for independence.

God has touched so many lives through your warm hugs and infectious giggle. Because of you, broken fences have been mended, and new friendships formed. I pray daily that God will use you to bring joy to others and will watch over you and guide you as only a loving Father can.

I love you more than I ever imagined possible, sweet baby. Thank you, God, for allowing me to be Jordan's mommy.

—Jennifer Deshler

# A Blessing for Baby

from _____

_____

_____

_____

_____

_____

_____

Bricks and mortar
make a house
but the laughter
of children
makes a home.

—Irish proverb

# A Blessing for Baby

from _____

_____

_____

_____

_____

_____

_____

hugs

words of praise

warm milk

laughter

love

friends

The best things in life are
the simple things.

family

giggles

B

fun

tickles

teddy bears

When a baby
comes into the world
it's as though the pure air
of heaven comes along.

—Johann Christoph Arnold

For rosy apples, juicy plums
And honey from the bees,
We thank you, heavenly Father God,
For such good gifts as these.

—Anonymous

# A Blessing for Baby

from_____

_____

_____

_____

_____

_____

# A Blessing for My Baby Girl

You are a pearl of great price, a treasure of great value. I look at your sweet, new face and beg God to put off forever the day when innocence will be replaced by the realities of life. May God who loves us so dearly grant me the privilege of gathering you close when you hurt, wiping your tears when you cry, and rejoicing out loud in your accomplishments. May our adventure together always be one of discovery, respect, deep affection and— most of all—love.

—Natalie Nichols Gillespie

# A Blessing for Baby

from_____

Lord, we long for our child,

Borne out of covenant love

Nurtured in love, hope, forgiveness,

Received as gift, blessing, joy.

—Barrowby

# A Blessing for Baby

from _____

_____

_____

_____

_____

_____

Two little eyes to look to God;

Two little ears to hear His word;

Two little feet to walk in His ways;

Two little lips to sing His praise;

Two little hands to do His will

And one little heart to love Him still.

—Welsh Proverb

# A Blessing for Baby

from_____

_____

_____

_____

_____

_____

Dear Father in heaven,

Look down from above;

Bless Father and Mother

And all

whom

I love.

—Anonymous

Children are
like daffodils.
Each year new ones
keep popping up.

—Barbara Jenkins

How precious…are Your thoughts to me, O God!
How great is the sum of them!
If I should count them, they would be more in number than the sand.

Psalm 139:17–18

# A Blessing for Baby

from _____

_____

_____

_____

_____

_____

_____

A Baby is to cuddle,
and rock,
and sing lullabies to,
and say goo, goo, goo to.

When the good Lord was creating fathers, He started with a tall frame.

An angel nearby said, "What kind of father is that? If you're going to make children so close to the ground, why have you put fathers up so high? He won't be able to shoot marbles without kneeling, tuck a child in bed without bending, or even kiss a child without a lot of stooping."

And God smiled and said, "Yes. But if I make him child-size, who would children have to look up to?"

—Erma Bombeck

# Words of Blessing for Baby

## What you are is:

P_____

R_____

E_____

C_____

I_____

O_____

U_____

S_____

He prayeth best who loveth best

All things both great and small;

For the dear God who loveth us,

He made and

loveth all.

—Samuel Taylor Coleridge

# A Blessing for Baby

from _____

Sweet dreams form a shade,

O're my lovely infant's head.

Sweet dreams of pleasant streams.

Be happy silent, moony beams.

—William Blake